Applying the Standards:
STEM
Grade 2

Credits
Content Editor: April Parker
Copy Editor: Nora Shoptaw

Visit *carsondellosa.com* for correlations to Common Core, state, national, and Canadian provincial standards.

Carson-Dellosa Publishing, LLC
PO Box 35665
Greensboro, NC 27425 USA
carsondellosa.com

ISBN 978-1-4838-1573-2
03-306151151

Table of Contents

Introduction

STEM education is a growing force in today's classroom. Exposure to science, technology, engineering, and math is important in twenty-first century learning as it allows students to succeed in higher education as well as a variety of careers.

While it can come in many forms, STEM education is most often presented as an engaging task that asks students to solve a problem. Additionally, creativity, collaboration, communication, and critical thinking are integral to every task. STEM projects are authentic learning tasks that guide students to address a variety of science and math standards. Also, students strengthen English Language Arts skills by recording notes and written reflections throughout the process.

In this book, students are asked to complete a range of tasks with limited resources. Materials for each task are limited to common household objects. Students are guided through each task by the steps of the engineering design process to provide a framework through which students can grow their comfort level and independently complete tasks.

Use the included rubric to guide assessment of student responses and further plan any necessary remediation. Confidence in STEM tasks will help students succeed in their school years and beyond.

Student Roles

Student collaboration is an important component of STEM learning. Encourage collaboration by having students complete tasks in groups. Teach students to communicate openly, support each other, and respect the contributions of all members. Keep in mind that collaborative grouping across achievement levels can provide benefits for all students as they pool various perspectives and experiences toward a group goal.

Consider assigning formal roles to students in each group. This will simplify the collaborative tasks needed to get a project done and done well. The basic roles of group structure are as follows:

- The *captain* leads and guides other students in their roles.

- The *guide* walks the team through the steps, keeps track of time, and encourages the team to try again.

- The *materials manager* gathers, organizes, and guides the use of materials.

- The *reporter* records the team's thoughts and reports on the final project to the class.

STEM Performance Rubric

Use this rubric as a guide for assessing students' project management skills. It can also be offered to students as a tool to show your expectations and scoring. Note: Some items may not apply to each project.

4	_____ Asks or identifies comprehensive high-level questions _____ Makes valid, nontrivial inferences based on evidence in the text _____ Uses an appropriate, complete strategy to solve the problem _____ Skillfully justifies the solution and strategy used _____ Offers insightful reasoning and strong evidence of critical thinking _____ Collaborates with others in each stage of the process _____ Effectively evaluates and organizes information and outcomes
3	_____ Asks or identifies ample high-level questions _____ Exhibits effective imagination and creativity _____ Uses an appropriate but incomplete strategy to solve the problem _____ Justifies answer and strategy used _____ Offers sufficient reasoning and evidence of critical thinking _____ Collaborates with others in most stages of the process _____ Evaluates and organizes some information or outcomes
2	_____ Asks or identifies a few related questions _____ Exhibits little imagination and creativity _____ Uses an inappropriate or unclear strategy for solving the problem _____ Attempts to justify answers and strategy used _____ Demonstrates some evidence of critical thinking _____ Collaborates with others if prompted _____ Can evaluate and organize simple information and outcomes
1	_____ Is unable to ask or identify pertinent questions _____ Does not exhibit adequate imagination and creativity _____ Uses no strategy or plan for solving the problem _____ Does not or cannot justify answer or strategy used _____ Demonstrates limited or no evidence of critical thinking _____ Does not collaborate with others _____ Cannot evaluate or organize information or outcomes

Name _____

Read the task. Then, follow the steps to complete the task.

Good Vibrations: Sound

Use cardboard boxes and rubber bands to create guitars that each make a different sound.

Materials

cardboard boxes
  (shoe box, tissue
  box, etc.)

a variety of rubber
  bands
scissors

Ask

What do you know? What do you need to know to get started?

_____

_____

Imagine

What could you do?

_____

_____

Plan

Choose an idea. Draw a model.

📓 Plan

What are your steps? Use your model to guide your plan.

_____

_____

_____

_____

⚒ Create

Follow your plan. What is working? Do you need to try something else?

_____

_____

🔄 Improve

How could you make it better?

_____

_____

💬 Communicate

How well did it work? Is the problem solved?

_____

_____

☀ Reflect

How did the length and size of the rubber bands make the sound different in each guitar?

_____

_____

_____

Name _____

Read the task. Then, follow the steps to complete the task.

Evaporation Station

Design a way to keep water from evaporating from a container.

Materials

aluminum foil   newspaper
fabric   paper or plastic cups
paper towels   water
plastic wrap

Ask

What do you know? What do you need to know to get started?

_____

_____

Imagine

What could you do?

_____

_____

Plan

Choose an idea. Draw a model.

📝 Plan

What are your steps? Use your model to guide your plan.

_____

_____

_____

_____

🖌️ Create

Follow your plan. What is working? Do you need to try something else?

_____

_____

🔄 Improve

How could you make it better?

_____

_____

💬 Communicate

How well did it work? Is the problem solved?

_____

_____

☀️ Reflect

Explain how your design stops evaporation.

_____

_____

_____

Name _____

Read the task. Then, follow the steps to complete the task.

Melting Pot: The States of Matter

Design the fastest way to melt ice.

Materials

aluminum foil
bowls (plastic,
   metal, glass, etc.)
ice cubes

ruler
timer
tin pie plate

Ask

What do you know? What do you need to know to get started?

_____

_____

Imagine

What could you do?

_____

_____

Plan

Choose an idea. Draw a model.

📓 Plan

What are your steps? Use your model to guide your plan.

_____

_____

_____

🔧 Create

Follow your plan. What is working? Do you need to try something else?

_____

_____

🔄 Improve

How could you make it better?

_____

_____

💬 Communicate

How well did it work? Is the problem solved?

_____

_____

☀ Reflect

How did the container the ice was in affect the melting time?

_____

_____

_____

Name _____

Read the task. Then, follow the steps to complete the task.

Cool My Home

Build a house that stays the coolest in direct sunlight.

Materials

aluminum foil
cardboard boxes,
   such as shoe
    boxes or tissue
    boxes
construction paper
cotton balls

paper milk cartons
newspaper
scissors
glue
tape
thermometer

 Ask

What do you know? What do you need to know to get started?

_____

_____

 Imagine

What could you do?

_____

_____

Plan

Choose an idea. Draw a model.

📝 Plan

What are your steps? Use your model to guide your plan.

_____

_____

_____

🛠 Create

Follow your plan. What is working? Do you need to try something else?

_____

_____

🔄 Improve

How could you make it better?

_____

_____

💬 Communicate

How well did it work? Is the problem solved?

_____

_____

☀ Reflect

How did the material used to build the house affect the temperature inside the house?

_____

_____

_____

Name _____

Read the task. Then, follow the steps to complete the task.

I'm a Meteorologist: Weather Tools

Create a tool a meteorologist could use to measure changes in the weather.

Materials

aluminum foil   straws
construction paper   craft sticks
cups (paper or   scissors
    plastic)   glue
pencils   tape
toothpicks

 Ask

What do you know? What do you need to know to get started?

_____

_____

☁ **Imagine**

What could you do?

_____

_____

📝 **Plan**

Choose an idea. Draw a model.

📝 Plan

What are your steps? Use your model to guide your plan.

_____

_____

_____

🔧 Create

Follow your plan. What is working? Do you need to try something else?

_____

_____

🔄 Improve

How could you make it better?

_____

_____

💬 Communicate

How well did it work? Is the problem solved?

_____

_____

☀ Reflect

How would a scientist use your tool to measure, record, or predict the weather?

_____

_____

_____

Name _____

Read the task. Then, follow the steps to complete the task.

Tower Buddy

Build a tower as tall as yourself that can stand on its own.

Materials

paper or plastic
  cups
paper milk cartons
paper towel rolls
wooden blocks
cardboard

straws
craft sticks
yardstick or
  meterstick
glue
tape

Ask

What do you know? What do you need to know to get started?

_____

_____

Imagine

What could you do?

_____

_____

Plan

Choose an idea. Draw a model.

📓 Plan

What are your steps? Use your model to guide your plan.

_____

_____

_____

🔧 Create

Follow your plan. What is working? Do you need to try something else?

_____

_____

🔄 Improve

How could you make it better?

_____

_____

💬 Communicate

How well did it work? Is the problem solved?

_____

_____

☀ Reflect

What strategy did you use to get the tower as tall as you are?

_____

_____

_____

Name _____

Read the task. Then, follow the steps to complete the task.

Batty Challenge: Measurement

Create a bat that has a wingspan that is exactly the same length as your own arm span.

Materials

construction paper
newspaper
ruler
string
straws
chenille stems

craft sticks
yardstick or
   meterstick
scissors
tape
glue

Ask

What do you know? What do you need to know to get started?

_____

_____

☁ Imagine

What could you do?

_____

_____

📝 Plan

Choose an idea. Draw a model.

📝 Plan

What are your steps? Use your model to guide your plan.

_____

_____

_____

🔧 Create

Follow your plan. What is working? Do you need to try something else?

_____

_____

🔄 Improve

How could you make it better?

_____

_____

💬 Communicate

How well did it work? Is the problem solved?

_____

_____

☀ Reflect

How did you check to see if your bat's wingspan was wide enough?

_____

_____

_____

Name _____

Read the task. Then, follow the steps to complete the task.

High in the Sky

Build a paper airplane that can travel across the room.

Materials

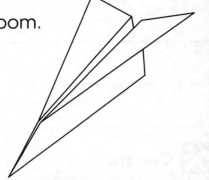

aluminum foil	wax paper
construction paper	paper clips
copy paper	scissors
markers	glue
straws	tape

 Ask

What do you know? What do you need to know to get started?

_____

_____

Imagine

What could you do?

_____

_____

Plan

Choose an idea. Draw a model.

📝 Plan

What are your steps? Use your model to guide your plan.

_____

_____

_____

_____

⚒️ Create

Follow your plan. What is working? Do you need to try something else?

_____

_____

🔄 Improve

How could you make it better?

_____

_____

💬 Communicate

How well did it work? Is the problem solved?

_____

_____

☀️ Reflect

What challenges did you have when making your airplane? How did you fix them?

_____

_____

_____

Name _____

Read the task. Then, follow the steps to complete the task.

Towering Heights

Using only the materials provided, create the tallest structure you can that stands on its own.

Materials

straws
scissors

24 inches (61 cm)
of tape

Ask

What do you know? What do you need to know to get started?

_____

_____

Imagine

What could you do?

_____

_____

Plan

Choose an idea. Draw a model.

Plan

What are your steps? Use your model to guide your plan.

_____

_____

_____

_____

Create

Follow your plan. What is working? Do you need to try something else?

_____

_____

Improve

How could you make it better?

_____

_____

Communicate

How well did it work? Is the problem solved?

_____

_____

Reflect

How did the base of your tower affect its height?

_____

_____

_____

Name _____

Read the task. Then, follow the steps to complete the task.

Home Sweet Home: Life Cycles

Create a home for a caterpillar that will meet all its changing needs.

Materials

a variety of bowls
cardboard boxes,
   such as shoe or
   tissue boxes
cotton balls
craft sticks
paper and plastic
   cups

dowel rods
glass jar
net fabric
paper milk cartons
a variety of rubber
   bands
glue
tape

 Ask

What do you know? What do you need to know to get started?

_____

_____

☁ **Imagine**

What could you do?

_____

_____

📝 **Plan**

Choose an idea. Draw a model.

📓 Plan

What are your steps? Use your model to guide your plan.

_____

_____

_____

_____

🛠️ Create

Follow your plan. What is working? Do you need to try something else?

_____

_____

🔄 Improve

How could you make it better?

_____

_____

💬 Communicate

How well did it work? Is the problem solved?

_____

_____

☀️ Reflect

How does the home you built meet all of the needs of a caterpillar?

_____

_____

_____

Name _____

Read the task. Then, follow the steps to complete the task.

In Hot Water

Figure out a way to heat water without electricity or fire.

Materials

aluminum foil
cups (paper or
   plastic)

thermometers
tin pie plate
water

 Ask

What do you know? What do you need to know to get started?

_____

_____

 Imagine

What could you do?

_____

_____

Plan

Choose an idea. Draw a model.

📓 Plan

What are your steps? Use your model to guide your plan.

_____

_____

_____

🛠️ Create

Follow your plan. What is working? Do you need to try something else?

_____

_____

🔄 Improve

How could you make it better?

_____

_____

💬 Communicate

How well did it work? Is the problem solved?

_____

_____

☀️ Reflect

How did you choose a heat source to warm the water? Why did you choose that heat source?

_____

_____

_____

Name _____

Read the task. Then, follow the steps to complete the task.

Vibrations Measure Up: Sound

Create an instrument that can make at least three different pitches.

Materials

cardboard boxes,
  such as shoe or
  tissue boxes
plastic bottles
a variety of rubber
  bands
string

pots and pans
a variety of spoons
straws
craft sticks
chenille stems
scissors

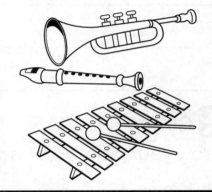

 Ask

What do you know? What do you need to know to get started?

_____

_____

Imagine

What could you do?

_____

_____

Plan

Choose an idea. Draw a model.

📓 Plan

What are your steps? Use your model to guide your plan.

_____

_____

_____

✂️ Create

Follow your plan. What is working? Do you need to try something else?

_____

_____

🔄 Improve

How could you make it better?

_____

_____

💬 Communicate

How well did it work? Is the problem solved?

_____

_____

☀️ Reflect

How did your design allow the instrument to make different pitches?

_____

_____

_____

Name _____

Read the task. Then, follow the steps to complete the task.

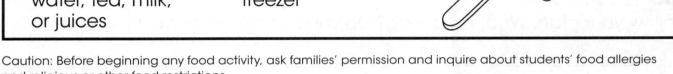

Ready, Set, Freeze: The States of Matter

Find a liquid that makes the best Popsicle.

Materials

paper or plastic
  cups
a variety of liquids,
  such as soda,
  water, tea, milk,
  or juices

craft sticks
tape
straws
thermometers
freezer

Caution: Before beginning any food activity, ask families' permission and inquire about students' food allergies and religious or other food restrictions.

 Ask

What do you know? What do you need to know to get started?

_____

_____

 Imagine

What could you do?

_____

_____

Plan

Choose an idea. Draw a model.

📓 Plan

What are your steps? Use your model to guide your plan.

_____

_____

_____

_____

🛠️ Create

Follow your plan. What is working? Do you need to try something else?

_____

_____

🔄 Improve

How could you make it better?

_____

_____

💬 Communicate

How well did it work? Is the problem solved?

_____

_____

🌟 Reflect

Which liquids worked best? Which worked worst? Explain your answers.

_____

_____

_____

Name _____

Read the task. Then, follow the steps to complete the task.

Get Wet

Find the best material for an umbrella.

Materials

construction paper   craft sticks
a variety of fabrics   water
newspaper   scissors
wax paper   glue
plastic wrap   tape
chenille stems

 Ask

What do you know? What do you need to know to get started?

_____

_____

Imagine

What could you do?

_____

_____

Plan

Choose an idea. Draw a model.

📓 Plan

What are your steps? Use your model to guide your plan.

_____

_____

_____

_____

🛠 Create

Follow your plan. What is working? Do you need to try something else?

_____

_____

🔄 Improve

How could you make it better?

_____

_____

💬 Communicate

How well did it work? Is the problem solved?

_____

_____

🌟 Reflect

What is most important about what you used to make your umbrella?

_____

_____

_____

Name _____

Read the task. Then, follow the steps to complete the task.

Bridging the Gap

Create a bridge that is at least 1 foot (30 cm) long and can support the weight of a toy car.

Materials

2 cups	toy car
straws	scissors
craft sticks	glue
toothpicks	tape
construction paper	

 Ask

What do you know? What do you need to know to get started?

_____

_____

Imagine

What could you do?

_____

_____

Plan

Choose an idea. Draw a model.

📝 Plan

What are your steps? Use your model to guide your plan.

_____

_____

_____

_____

🔧 Create

Follow your plan. What is working? Do you need to try something else?

_____

_____

🔄 Improve

How could you make it better?

_____

_____

💬 Communicate

How well did it work? Is the problem solved?

_____

_____

☀ Reflect

What one additional item could you add to the list if you wanted to build a bridge that was at least 1 yard (1 m) long?

_____

_____

_____

Name _____

Read the task. Then, follow the steps to complete the task.

Create a Cloud: The Water Cycle

Create an environment where a cloud could form.

Materials

aluminum foil
paper or plastic
  cups
bowls
plastic bags

plastic container
  with a lid
plastic wrap
thermometer
tin pie plate
water

Ask

What do you know? What do you need to know to get started?

_____

_____

Imagine

What could you do?

_____

_____

Plan

Choose an idea. Draw a model.

📓 Plan

What are your steps? Use your model to guide your plan.

_____

_____

_____

🔧 Create

Follow your plan. What is working? Do you need to try something else?

_____

_____

🔄 Improve

How could you make it better?

_____

_____

💬 Communicate

How well did it work? Is the problem solved?

_____

_____

☀️ Reflect

Explain how you made a cloud form.

_____

_____

_____

Name _____

Read the task. Then, follow the steps to complete the task.

Cooking with the Sun: Energy

Prove or disprove whether you could bake a cookie on a sidewalk.

Materials

aluminum foil	paper towels
bowls	spoons
cookie dough	tin pie plate

Caution: Before beginning any food activity, ask families' permission and inquire about students' food allergies and religious or other restrictions.

Ask

What do you know? What do you need to know to get started?

_____

_____

Imagine

What could you do?

_____

_____

Plan

Choose an idea. Draw a model.

📓 Plan

What are your steps? Use your model to guide your plan.

_____

_____

_____

_____

🛠 Create

Follow your plan. What is working? Do you need to try something else?

_____

_____

🔄 Improve

How could you make it better?

_____

_____

💬 Communicate

How well did it work? Is the problem solved?

_____

_____

🌟 Reflect

How can the sun's energy be used for cooking food?

_____

_____

_____

Name _____

Read the task. Then, follow the steps to complete the task.

Sound Can Really Move

Design a way to play music so that everyone in the next room can hear the music clearly without changing the volume.

Materials

aluminum foil	newspaper
music player with	paper cups
external speakers	string
or radio	scissors

Ask

What do you know? What do you need to know to get started?

_____

_____

Imagine

What could you do?

_____

_____

Plan

Choose an idea. Draw a model.

📓 Plan

What are your steps? Use your model to guide your plan.

_____

_____

_____

_____

🔧 Create

Follow your plan. What is working? Do you need to try something else?

_____

_____

🔄 Improve

How could you make it better?

_____

_____

💬 Communicate

How well did it work? Is the problem solved?

_____

_____

☀️ Reflect

How did you get the sound to travel to the next room?

_____

_____

_____

Name _____

Read the task. Then, follow the steps to complete the task.

A Solid Tower

Use solid objects to form the tallest tower possible.

Materials

a variety of solid
   objects, such as
   wooden blocks,
   books, or cans

Ask

What do you know? What do you need to know to get started?

_____

_____

Imagine

What could you do?

_____

_____

Plan

Choose an idea. Draw a model.

📝 Plan

What are your steps? Use your model to guide your plan.

_____

_____

_____

⚒ Create

Follow your plan. What is working? Do you need to try something else?

_____

_____

🔄 Improve

How could you make it better?

_____

_____

💬 Communicate

How well did it work? Is the problem solved?

_____

_____

☀ Reflect

What types of solid objects worked best to form a tall tower? Why?

_____

_____

_____

Name _____

Read the task. Then, follow the steps to complete the task.

Bubbles Down Under: The States of Matter

Find a way to create bubbles under water.

Materials

bowls
cups
water

plastic containers
  with lids

Ask

What do you know? What do you need to know to get started?

_____

_____

Imagine

What could you do?

_____

_____

Plan

Choose an idea. Draw a model.

📝 Plan

What are your steps? Use your model to guide your plan.

_____

_____

_____

🔧 Create

Follow your plan. What is working? Do you need to try something else?

_____

_____

🔄 Improve

How could you make it better?

_____

_____

💬 Communicate

How well did it work? Is the problem solved?

_____

_____

☀ Reflect

How does air behave under water?

_____

_____

_____

Name _____

Read the task. Then, follow the steps to complete the task.

Weighty Balloons: Measurement

Design a way to measure the weight of air.

Materials

balloons   tape
dowel   scale
string

Caution: Before beginning any balloon activity, ask families about possible latex allergies. Also remember that uninflated or popped balloons may present a choking hazard.

Ask

What do you know? What do you need to know to get started?

_____

_____

Imagine

What could you do?

_____

_____

Plan

Choose an idea. Draw a model.

📝 Plan

What are your steps? Use your model to guide your plan.

_____

_____

_____

_____

⚒️ Create

Follow your plan. What is working? Do you need to try something else?

_____

_____

🔄 Improve

How could you make it better?

_____

_____

💬 Communicate

How well did it work? Is the problem solved?

_____

_____

☀️ Reflect

How do you know air has weight?

_____

_____

_____

Name _____

Read the task. Then, follow the steps to complete the task.

The Better to Hear You With: Sound

Create a device that can allow you to talk to someone in another room.

Materials

construction paper   straws
craft sticks   string
cups   scissors
newspaper   glue
plastic wrap   tape

 Ask

What do you know? What do you need to know to get started?

_____

_____

Imagine

What could you do?

_____

_____

Plan

Choose an idea. Draw a model.

📝 Plan

What are your steps? Use your model to guide your plan.

_____

_____

_____

🔧 Create

Follow your plan. What is working? Do you need to try something else?

_____

_____

🔄 Improve

How could you make it better?

_____

_____

💬 Communicate

How well did it work? Is the problem solved?

_____

_____

☀ Reflect

How is your creation similar to the human ear?

_____

_____

_____

Name _____

Read the task. Then, follow the steps to complete the task.

Meet the Band

Create an instrument that uses moving air to make sound.

Materials

plastic or glass bottles	glue
construction paper	paper towel rolls
	tape

Ask

What do you know? What do you need to know to get started?

_____

_____

Imagine

What could you do?

_____

_____

Plan

Choose an idea. Draw a model.

📝 Plan

What are your steps? Use your model to guide your plan.

_____

_____

_____

🛠 Create

Follow your plan. What is working? Do you need to try something else?

_____

_____

🔄 Improve

How could you make it better?

_____

_____

💬 Communicate

How well did it work? Is the problem solved?

_____

_____

☀ Reflect

How does moving air create sound in the instrument?

_____

_____

_____

Name _____

Read the task. Then, follow the steps to complete the task.

Building the Pyramids: Geometry

Build a pyramid that is made of objects you can find around your home or classroom.

Materials

construction paper
craft sticks
chenille stems
cups (paper or
  plastic)
glue

newspaper
scissors
straws
sugar cubes
tape

Caution: Before beginning any food activity, ask families' permission and inquire about students' food allergies and religious or other restrictions.

 Ask

What do you know? What do you need to know to get started?

_____

_____

 Imagine

What could you do?

_____

_____

Plan

Choose an idea. Draw a model.

📓 Plan

What are your steps? Use your model to guide your plan.

_____

_____

_____

🔧 Create

Follow your plan. What is working? Do you need to try something else?

_____

_____

🔄 Improve

How could you make it better?

_____

_____

💬 Communicate

How well did it work? Is the problem solved?

_____

_____

🔆 Reflect

How were triangles an important part of your pyramid?

_____

_____

_____

Name _____

Read the task. Then, follow the steps to complete the task.

Flights of Fancy

Design an airplane that can travel at least 25 feet (about 7.5 meters).

Materials

newspaper	scissors
copy paper	tape
paper clips	glue

Ask

What do you know? What do you need to know to get started?

_____

_____

Imagine

What could you do?

_____

_____

Plan

Choose an idea. Draw a model.

📓 Plan

What are your steps? Use your model to guide your plan.

_____

_____

_____

_____

⚒ Create

Follow your plan. What is working? Do you need to try something else?

_____

_____

🔄 Improve

How could you make it better?

_____

_____

💬 Communicate

How well did it work? Is the problem solved?

_____

_____

✹ Reflect

How did weight affect your airplane's flight?

_____

_____

_____

Name _____

Read the task. Then, follow the steps to complete the task.

Highs and Lows: Pitch

Use materials around your home or classroom to create and record the highest- and lowest-pitched sounds you can.

Materials

drinking glasses
glass jar
recording device,
   such as an
   electronic tablet,
   cell phone, or
   computer

balloons
bottles
spoons
straws
string
tape
water

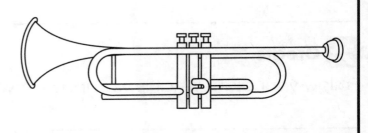

Caution: Before beginning any balloon activity, ask families about possible latex allergies. Also, remember that uninflated or popped balloons may present a choking hazard.

 Ask

What do you know? What do you need to know to get started?

_____

_____

 Imagine

What could you do?

_____

_____

Plan

Choose an idea. Draw a model.

✎ Plan

What are your steps? Use your model to guide your plan.

_____

_____

_____

✂ Create

Follow your plan. What is working? Do you need to try something else?

_____

_____

↻ Improve

How could you make it better?

_____

_____

💬 Communicate

How well did it work? Is the problem solved?

_____

_____

☀ Reflect

How did the type of item you used make a difference in the sound?

_____

_____

_____

Name _____

Read the task. Then, follow the steps to complete the task.

The Juice Mystery: Evaporation

Make the juice evaporate out of a piece of fruit.

Materials

craft sticks
plastic wrap
sliced fruit, such as
   apples,
   pineapples, or
   oranges

straws
string
tin pie plate
toothpicks

Caution: Before beginning any food activity, ask families' permission and inquire about students' food allergies and religious or other restrictions.

Ask

What do you know? What do you need to know to get started?

_____

_____

Imagine

What could you do?

_____

_____

Plan

Choose an idea. Draw a model.

📓 Plan

What are your steps? Use your model to guide your plan.

_____

_____

_____

🔧 Create

Follow your plan. What is working? Do you need to try something else?

_____

_____

🔄 Improve

How could you make it better?

_____

_____

💬 Communicate

How well did it work? Is the problem solved?

_____

_____

☀️ Reflect

How did the juice turn into another form of matter?

_____

_____

_____

Name _____

Read the task. Then, follow the steps to complete the task.

Steam Machine: The States of Matter

Find a way to create steam without using a stove or microwave.

Materials

aluminum foil	thermometer
ice cubes	tin pie plate
pots and pans	water

Ask

What do you know? What do you need to know to get started?

_____

_____

Imagine

What could you do?

_____

_____

Plan

Choose an idea. Draw a model.

📝 Plan

What are your steps? Use your model to guide your plan.

_____

_____

_____

_____

🛠 Create

Follow your plan. What is working? Do you need to try something else?

_____

_____

🔄 Improve

How could you make it better?

_____

_____

💬 Communicate

How well did it work? Is the problem solved?

_____

_____

🌟 Reflect

Why is temperature important in making steam?

_____

_____

_____

Name _____

Read the task. Then, follow the steps to complete the task.

Ooey Gooey: The States of Matter

Create a substance that has both the properties of a liquid and a solid.

Materials

bowls	plastic containers
cornstarch	salt
flour	spoons
glue	water
gelatin	

Caution: Before beginning any food activity, ask families' permission and inquire about students' food allergies and religious or other restrictions.

Ask

What do you know? What do you need to know to get started?

_____

_____

Imagine

What could you do?

_____

_____

Plan

Choose an idea. Draw a model.

✎ Plan

What are your steps? Use your model to guide your plan.

_____

_____

_____

✂ Create

Follow your plan. What is working? Do you need to try something else?

_____

_____

↻ Improve

How could you make it better?

_____

_____

💬 Communicate

How well did it work? Is the problem solved?

_____

_____

☀ Reflect

Why is your creation not just a solid?

_____

_____

_____

Name _____

Read the task. Then, follow the steps to complete the task.

The Model Ear

Design a model that represents the human ear.

Materials

bowls	paper plates
construction paper	plastic bags
paper or plastic	plastic wrap
cups	a variety of rubber
fabric	bands
newspaper	tape

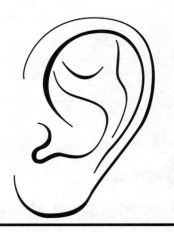

 Ask

What do you know? What do you need to know to get started?

_____

_____

Imagine

What could you do?

_____

_____

Plan

Choose an idea. Draw a model.

📓 Plan

What are your steps? Use your model to guide your plan.

_____

_____

_____

_____

✂️ Create

Follow your plan. What is working? Do you need to try something else?

_____

_____

🔄 Improve

How could you make it better?

_____

_____

💬 Communicate

How well did it work? Is the problem solved?

_____

_____

☀️ Reflect

How is vibration important in your model?

_____

_____

_____